# NATURAL ORDER

# NATURAL ORDER

## VISUAL ARTS & CRAFTS
## IN
## GRIZEDALE FOREST PARK

Editor
Bill Grant

Picture credits:
page 1 - Val Corbett; frontispiece - Bill Grant; page 6 - Val Corbett; page 16 - Val Corbett;
page 18 - Bill Grant; page 19 - Wendy Brown by Bill Grant, Peter Lloyd by Val Corbett,
Riven Seat by Mike Oram; page 20/21 - Bill Grant; page 24 - Val Corbett;
page 26 - Val Corbett; page 29 Val Corbett; page 32 - Carol Tyler; page 38 - Val Corbett

*Special thanks go to Hamish Macfarlane*
*for his constant enthusiasm*
*and practical support for this book*

Hilda Newton for perserverance and dedication

First published 1996 by
The Grizedale Society
Grizedale
Nr Hawkshead
Ambleside
Cumbria LA22 0QJ


ISBN 0 9525450 5 5

Editorial Consultant   Paul Harris, Whittingehame House, Haddington, Scotland
Design by Silva Sever
Printed by Gorenjski tisk
in The Republic of Slovenia

# CONTENTS

# INTRODUCTION

*"A workshop to be managed for many purposes under a plan for balanced use"*

Ruskin

The launch of Visual Arts UK 1996 seemed a propitious time to produce "Natural Order". This book deals with the multiplicity of art forms but especially the Visual Arts which co-exist in Grizedale Forest Park, hand-in-hand with the commercial production forest.

The Grizedale Society, a registered charity was founded in 1969, partly in response to the highly succesful outdoor recreational plan which Forest Enterprise had pioneered between 1963 and 1968, but mainly as a result of a Winston Churchill Fellowship awarded to Bill Grant in 1968.

This led to the founding of the Theatre in the Forest, an intimate multimedia venue, promoting classical music, jazz, drama, dance, natural history, film shows etc. The Theatre is the 'body politic' of the Society, providing the administrative back-up to the other art forms which have since evolved.

In 1977, with the Theatre well established, at the suggestion of Peter Davies of Nothern Arts, we initiated Sculpture in the Landscape. This project, based on artists' residencies, started slowly; it was difficult to overcome the natural antipathy of the local population, who made life rather difficult for the first few sculptors. After all, they hade never been exposed to contemporary sculpture before. However, as the locals slowly grew more understanding, sculptors and their work were more readily accepted. In time, the response by the general public steadily grew, and helped by a good deal of unsolicited media attention, the project matured.

The fascination of sculpture at Grizedale results directly from the artist's empathy with the forest environment. Work is not specifically "commissioned". Once carefully selected, artists are given complete artistic freedom. Above all, we give them time - time to select a site - time to design their work and submit a proposal. The final monitoring of the artistic content is made at the point of proposal. All of the work is site-specific, made on site and belonging organically to the location, complementing the forest background, rather than competing with it. Thus it avoids the aggression often associated with work sited in the built environment.

Residencies are awarded not only to established artists, both national and international, but critical attention is paid to young up and coming sculptors, who demonstrate creative potential. Addressing the needs of, and providing opportunities for young artists, is an essential part of our rationale. Taking risks is part of our lifestyle. Otherwise, how do we find the new Goldsworthys ?

This policy, adopted in the early days, discovered not only Goldsworthy, (who was still in college when the project started), but it also found Kemp, Harris, Mathews, Frost, Ryder and a host of others, most of whom are now household names. The Sculpture project has now become dynamic with work being removed each year and new sculptures added.

Craftworkers and painters work within similar parameters. Unlike sculptors who leave all of their work behind, seiling exhibitions are arranged for crafts and painting which is an added bonus for the resident artists. In common with the sculptors their work reflects their affinity with a new found environment, fresh initiatives are discovered and new techniques developed.

Grizedale forest is now visited by some 350,000 day visitors annually and artists frequently find themselves at the sharp end of an inquiring public. The ensuing debate between sculptors, craftsworkers and painters and the public, is both persuasive and interpretative.

An important facet of the Residencies is the invitation to attend the great variety of theatre events and seats are always made available free as an integral part of their residential experience.

The main trust of Grizedale is that of an unique holistic arts complex located in that most rural of situations a 9,500 acre forest - with no public transport - yet people beat a path to it. It features prominently on the curriculum of, and is visited by universities, polytechnics, schools, colleges of education and art etc., who use it as a role model.

The work of the Grizedale Society has been recognised by many awards and accolades, too numerous to mention. The methods of presentation and the manifold versatility of the work and the fusing of art with nature is having a profound influence on public attitudes towards contemporary art.

All of the contributors to this book, like the sculpture, are "site related"! They have all worked with, for, or in Grizedale over the last two decades and more. They are most gratefully acknowledged.

Thanks are also due to Nothern Arts for their financial support and the confidence they have shown in our work. Likewise, we are more than grateful to Cumbria County Council and South Lakeland District Council for their much valued help.

Above all we salute the artists of all disciplines who have made Grizedale so exciting - so innovative and so accessible.

Two major initiatives for 1996 are designed to take the Society forward into the twenty first century. For the last two decades we have struggled with inadequate rented accommodation for artists.

After two and a half years of searching and negotiation, an ideal solution has been found. A vernacular farmhouse with a unique "Cruck" barn, suitable for seminars and small conferences, together with a two-bedroomed service flat, have been secured with the help of the National Lottery.

This has only been possible with matching money from contingency funds built up over many years at considerable personal sacrifice within the Society.

Close to this new environmental base, arrangements have been finalised with Forest Enterprise to enable the Society to design an International Woodland Sculpture Trail, involving sculptors mainly from Pacific Rim and South American countries. This high profile trail will underpin the already established international reputation of the Grizedale Society and offer further opportunities to the public for a more innovative and highly accessible art experience.

This base will ensure that sculptors, crafts people, painters and performing artists can be accommodated in high quality accommodation in surroundings of unrivalled natural beauty.

Herein lies the realisation of a dream.

W. Grant
Director

# FOREWORD

*"Sculpture is an art of the open air. Daylight, sunlight is necessary to it, and for me its best setting and complement is nature. I would rather have a piece of my sculpture put in a landscape, than in, or on, the most beautiful building I know."*
*Henry Moore, 1951.*

There aren't any Henry Moores at Grizedale - and some might breathe a sigh of relief about that - but the spirit of Moore's words strongly informs the ethos there. Until Moore came along few, if any, artists were interested in exhibiting work outdoors as a matter of course. The history of sculpture made specifically for open-air display begins after 1945 with the shows of sculpture in parks inaugurated at Battersea in 1948. Of course, works of art had been placed outside before then, in the form of statuary, war memorials and the sculpted facades of buildings both secular and religious, but an art which had no directly commemorative, symbolic or narrative function had not previously existed. Art for art's sake, especially where open air sculpture is concerned, is a very recent phenomenon indeed.

Exhibitions like those at Battersea and, later, in Regent's Park, continue today in assorted venues around the country, and have given rise to the comparatively recent flowering of sculpture parks. Among the original aims of sculpture parks was to make it easier for the public to see art without having to suffer the intimidation of entering an art gallery. All those porticoes and posh accents, all that reverential silence... Open air sculpture was seen to be doing away with all that supposed élitist nonsense. In the post-war, populist world in which art was deemed 'good for you', if the people were too cowed to come to it, it had to be taken to them. Open air sculpture was a way of making art relevant to everyday life because that was the situation in which it was being seen. This tendency has been reinforced more recently by the growth in 'public art', the manifestations of which are now - courtesy of assorted state-funded organisations - regularly deposited on our pavements, precincts and squares. I am bound to say that with the introduction of lottery money, public sculpture in urban settings looks destined to reach the epidemic proportions of a plague.

The increase of sculpture in the open has coincided with the evolution of 'green' movements throughout the world and, more specifically, with a respect for nature (especially among younger artists) which in its reverence comes close to a religion. Whereas once the closure of a factory or a pit caused demonstrations, nothing, it seems, is as likely to inspire public anger and mobilise action than the destruction of a wood or cruelty to animals. This renewed respect for the natural world, with which the overwhelming majority are in full sympathy, is about the closest we come in contemporary life to having a collective sense of belief in something important. Perhaps this accounts for the success of Grizedale because this theme of preserving and conserving the rural environment from further despoliation is one which underscores the work of many artists producing sculpture for pastoral settings. Given this consensus it could be argued that the worship of nature has replaced Christianity as the principal bond binding people together in the late 20th century. In many ways Grizedale is the cathedral of this new religion. I felt it appropriate the first time I walked around the Silurian Way through the forest, to imagine John Ruskin, who lived nearby and for whom nature was the face of God, venturing hereabouts on solitary, contemplative walks looking for subjects to paint.

Artists from all over the world are invited to work at Grizedale. They arrive like so many pilgrims and many talk of their residencies as representing a sort of retreat. They don't bring works with them, dump them in the forest and then escape back to their city studios. Instead, they arrive and work in the woods with the materials that come to hand there. Thus, the place itself is allowed to dictate at least in part what they do. Artists are neither invasive nor dictatorial and the effect one gets walking around is of immense respect on their part. To impose permanence on a commercial forest which changes and regenerates daily would demonstrably be the wrong approach to take. In consequence, most of the works are made from wood, stone or slate which will, like the forest itself, decay and collapse back into the earth to be re-absorbed into the material fund from which other things will grow or be constructed. Other pieces have been designed to grow and change along with their surroundings.

What has struck me during my visits to Grizedale, despite the uniform sympathy of artistic approach, is the impressive diversity of sculptures produced. Some are jokey and entertaining, others are grandly architectural like the forest itself. Nearly all are ingenious and many are beautifully, delicately made. Some are vast enclosures or stockades while others are small, subtle and so remote they are hard to find. I felt a special poignancy and pleasure at not being able to locate some of the work. In echoing the appearance of their immediate or distant surroundings, many pieces give the impression of being specifically tied to this place. They would simply not work anywhere else.

Grizedale is special. It combines my two favourite interests; walking in and observing nature; and looking at an artist's original and sensitively made responses to the world in which we all live. It is astonishing how Grizedale has, in such a short time, made such a big impact on the artistic community and it is no surprise that foreign arts administrators flock there in order to see how a sculpture park might best be organised.

David Lee
Editor, Art Review
March, 1996

# ART IN THE LANDSCAPE

## VICKY SLOWE

Less than three hundred years ago, the lakes and mountains of Cumberland and Westmorland were not regarded as having any special significance save as a wild, barren, inhospitable and deserted waste land, which was better avoided. The physical features were known to exist, but repelled rather than attracted attention.

That which repels one generation frequently attracts the admiring attention of the next. Such quantum shifts of attitude characterise the history of the cultural appreciation of Lakeland scenery.

Some framework for the better understanding of such changes in taste can be gained by applying the theories first developed in the middle ages by continental scholars, especially by the monk Curtuis. Curtuis - inevitably - took a Christian stance and tried to categorise landscape in Biblical terms. He easily identified the two opposite extremes; the fertile, productive, sheltered, fruitful, beautiful, luxurious, easy Garden, (alias: Eden, paradise, arcadia, utopia, shangri-la), where man finds rest, order, wholeness, unity, restoration and healing, versus the untamed, uncontrollable, terrifying, dangerous, chaotic, alien wilderness, (originally a landscape of natural disorder, beyond the creation or control of people), where the damned are lost, the saved are redeemed, the strong are tested.

Between these two poles, literally occupying the central ground which was neither one thing nor the other, lay the Middlelandscape, which the spin - doctors of the day could transform, through artifice and fashion, to near garden or near Wilderness, at whim. The Middlelandscape was where landscape's image could be manipulated.

Garden and Wilderness were not simply Judaeo - Christian traditions, however.

Various civilisations - classical Greek and Roman, Arab, Indian, Chinese, Japanese - had developed the garden as private, personal territory, safe, ordered, designed, and groomed and raked to perfection. The same cultures recognised wilder lands as the place for adventure, terror, spiritual torment, Christian scholars simply adapted existing, widespread ideas to their own ends.

The late 20th. century has compounded the paradox. In contemporary usage, the term Wilderness denotes places of great unspoiled beauty, (which is ironic in this period of steadily declining faith. For, in Biblical terms, Wildernesses can be miraculously converted into Gardens when the lost souls find direction and purpose).

During the first half of the 18th. century, the picturesque discovery of the lakes and mountains of Cumberland and Westmorland coincided, in the national consciousness, with the identification of an unique place - the Lake District and the metamorphosis of that place, which became synonymous with all that was best in landscape scenery. This ranged from unsought wilderness via Middlelandscape to (briefly) idyllic Garden, before a lengthy limbo in the realms of Middlelandscape, where, despite the best - or worst - efforts of the managing agencies, (The National Trust, The Lake District National Park Authority, Forest Enterprise), it remains.

Then, as now, that quality of uniqueness embraced a distinct unity of natural landscape and cultural scenery, which John Ruskin, 1819 - 1900, (in "The Stones of Venice: The Nature of Gothic"), described as "this look of mountain brotherhood between cathedral and the Alp".

Daniel Defoe and Celia Fiennes, in the 17th century, may have shuddered vicariously over the "horrid" precipices at the edge of the mountain passes and fretted over the poor, tumbledown dwellings of the native Cumbrians, but, less than a century later, the Romantics of the 18th. century traversed the mountains with equanimity and saw the vernacular buildings as fit homes for the Arcadian "confraternity of shepherds", who epitomised that ideal oneness of man with nature extolled by Jean Jaques Rousseau, and later by Wordsworth and the Lake Poets.

In the early years of the 18th. century, wealthy men of property, who had received a classical education and who had taken the Grand Tour to see "the glory that was Greece and the splendour that was Rome",  took  art as a reference point for landscape and garden designs, and began to extend the garden into their parkland, out into the landscape.

"Art" in this context meant the paintings for Claude Gellee, usually known as Claude Lorraine, 1600-1682,  who used "the later mannerist traditions of the division of the picture into areas of dark greenish-brown foreground, light green middle distance, and blue far distance, with the composition set out in coulisses[2] to create a sense of infinite distance, and tree forms treated as feathery fronds in silhouette". Claude developed the landscape of mood, first explored by the German painter, Adam Elsheimer, 1578-161-, creating poetic lighting effects by looking into the sun in a blaze of golden light. His celebrated "golden glow" shimmered on water to magical effect and drenched his painted world in the light and confidence of the Hellenistic imagination : the gods are like ourselves, only more beautiful, and descend to earth to teach man reason and the laws of harmony.

There was an evolutionary progression from the artist's landscape of the imagination via the gardener's landscaped park to the connoisseur's growing interest in the natural landscape.

At first, the natural landscapes which were the most admired were those that looked just like a picture by Claude, or Gaspar Poussin.  Such landscapes were termed "picturesque", in tribute.  But this original meaning was swiftly reversed, and a "Picturesque Landscape" rapidly came to mean a scene pictorially worthy of immediate transfer to canvas.  The phrase soon gained a derogatory implication, which is still current ; amongst many which believe themselves sophisticated.

The emergence of "The Picturesque" established a new type of beauty, midway between Burke's "Sublime" and the "Beautiful", (basically, pretty). The effect of "The Picturesque" depended on roughness, irregularity, and, to a certain extent, deformity.

Because those interested in viewing the natural landscape were used to seeing it in framed pictures, they experienced great difficulties in picking out, with the naked eye, those features most worthy of admiration from amongst the generalities. Artists were no longer exerting editorial control, and their patrons were lost without such direction.

The entrepreneurs soon marketed suitable solutions to this problem. Guide book writers devised tours linking the best view points, identifying the best "stations", (where to stand, which direction to face, which features to observe at which times of day), from which "tourists" would obtain the best views, thus setting tastes. Optical instrument makers designed the "landscape mirror", often referred to as a "Claude glass"; these were slightly convex, blackened mirrors which Father Thomas West, in his pioneering Guide to the Lakes, (first published in 1778, but in circulation in manuscript form from about 1760), describes as " of glass of 4 to 4.5 inches in diameter which should be the segment of a large circle, otherwise distant and small objects are not perceived in them. To use them, the traveller must turn his back on the scene and look in his mirror for a clear view ..."

Such mirrors literally framed a digestible, manageable, postcard - sized if somewhat dim reflection of the view, in much the same manner as the viewfinder of a camera. It has been plausibly suggested that this "through a glass darkly" view of landscape contributed to the dull tones of mid - 18th. century water colours.

Silvered mirrors were used on days too dark for the blackened kind. The landscape could also be viewed through coloured filters, used separately or in combination to alter mood or season or weather. The most sophisticated version of this approach was to be found in the stained glass fitted into the bay window of the station, the elegant pleasure-house erected on Claife Heights, on the west shore of Windermere, above the ferry crossing, on the site recognised by Father West as "the pride of the Lakes; the ruins of the walls remain, but the rose and amber and russet and storm-black glass has long gone."

The cult of the picturesque thus set "rules of viewing and experiencing" the landscape, controlling what was seen and contriving how it was seen, and therefore taming the "Wilderness into a Middlelandscape for about forty years from C. 1750 until the turn of the century.

In the latter years of the 18th. century, the growing influence of French - particularly Rousseau's - philosophy, and then of Wordsworth's poetry, tipped the balance of the Lake District's Middlelandscape in favour of the polarity of the Garden.

The genius who catalysed this transformation was Rousseau, who seeking refuge from persecution on an island in the Lake of Bienne, became so absorbed in "the flux and reflux of the waves"[3] that he became completely at one with nature, lost all consciousness of an independent self,[4] "forgot all painful memories of the past or anxieties about the future,"[5] and knew nothing but "the sense of being"[6], thus realising "that our existence is nothing  but a succession of moments perceived through the senses."[7]

This shift - in the midst of the Age of Reason - from Descartes' "I think therefore I am" to Rousseau's "I feel therefore I am" caused a revolution in human feeling, developing a new cult of sensibility.

Rousseau's belief in the beauty and innocence of nature was expanded into a major philosophical work, his Discourse on the Origin of inequality, which propounded the idea that natural man was virtuous; "the noble savage" was observed in Tahiti and briefly discovered by the cognoscenti to be living a happy and harmonious life in the wilderness that encompassed the lakes and mountains of Cumberland and Westmorland, which was thus transubstantiated into a garden, an English paradise.

Nature became the new religion, but its prophets emphasised different aspects. Rousseau's The Social Contract was to become "the gospel of revolution"[8], Goethe's vision of "all living things as striving for fuller development through an infinitely long process of adaptation"[9] inspired Darwin and the theory of evolution, but the purely inspirational approach of the English Romantic poets, Coleridge and Wordsworth, shaped attitudes to landscape appreciation.

Coleridge found in nature a a highly mystical transcendental experience, later re-created through hallucinatory drugs, whilst Wordsworth added a moral dimension, recognising that "simple people and animals often show more courage and loyalty and unselfishness than sophisticated people, and also a greater sense of wholeness of life :

> "One impulse from a vernal wood
> May teach you more of man
> Of moral evil and of good
> Than all the sages can"

> " Sweet is the lore which nature brings;
> Our meddling intellect
> Mis-shapes the beauteous form of things :-
> We murder to dissect"[10]

This mystic communion with nature in the Lakeland Garden attracted ever increasing numbers of "tourists" eager to share the experience, and well meaning attempts to control and manage the influx so as not to destroy the phenomenon quickly reduced the Lake District to being, once again, the archetypal Middlelandscape.

John Ruskin, the great arbiter of Victorian taste, shared Wordsworth's exaltation in the grandeur of mountain scenery, but delved beneath the surface of all things - whether paintings, buildings, or mountains - for their symbolic significance.   Ruskin differed from Wordsworth in possessing the investigative curiosity of the true scientist.   In Modern Painters, Volume III, Ruskin claimed that "the chief narrowness of Wordsworth's mind" lay in his inability to understand that "to break a rock with a hammer in search of crystal may sometimes be an act not disgraceful to human nature, and that to dissect a flower may sometimes be as proper as to dream over it;  whereas all experience goes to teach us, that among men of average intellect the most äuseful members of society are the dissectors, not the dreamers."[10]

It was Wordsworth, though, who first suggested that the Lake District was a sort of national property belonging to all with the eyes and hearts to see, and it was Ruskin who developed the idea, becoming the eminence grise who inspired Canon H.D. Rawnsley and Octavia Hill, both his acolytes, to found The National Trust for the Preservation of Ancient Buildings and places of outstanding natural beauty.   Ruskin was also behind the national parks movement, the green belt, garden cities, the clean air acts; a man of ideas, he let others implement them.

It is no wonder then that any resident of or visitor to the Lake District carries an excess of both conscious and sub-conscious cultural and environmental baggage when they gaze at this particular landscape of memory.

The challenge for any artist working at Grizedale is to build on this collective memory - and say something new.

## REFERENCES

1. Murray, Peter and Linda, A Dictionary of Art and Artists, Penguin Reference Books, 1971.

2. Coulisse : French for the wings of the stage.   The term is used in art history to describe the type of composition where the optical illusion of distance is created by leading the eye back into depth by overlapping features, usually alternately left and right, such as bushes, trees, hills, winding rivers.

3. Clark, Kenneth, Civilisation, Chapter II, "The Worship of Nature", discusses the impact of Rousseau, Goethe, the Lake poets and the Romantic movement, with great clarity, (British Broadcasting Corporation and John Murray, London, 1969).

4. Ibid

5. Ibid

6 Ibid

7. Ibid

8. Ibid

9. Ibid

10. Ibid

# CRAFTS

MEG FALCONER

In 1987 another episode in the Grizedale saga began. This time it was the formation of residencies for craftspeople. The vision and perception of the Grizedale Society was applied to save the old saw mill building at the centre of the Grizedale complex for re-structuring into a gallery. The intention previously being demolition in favour of more car parking spaces.

Leased from the Forestry Commission for a perpercorn rent, it was subsequently transformed into "The Gallery-in-the Forest", with money raised from various trusts and foundations.

The Gallery conversion created the opportunity to rebuild the large, delapidated "lean-to" at its rear. The Crafts workshop was thus constructed and equipped with woodworking machinery grant aided by the Crafts Council.

The Gallery was opened in 1988, and now houses an ongoing didactic exhibition of working drawings, sculpture, maquettes and photographs, relating to sculpture in the forest, which gives the public an insight into the sculptor's working process. The Grizedale collection of wood-related craftwork is on permanent display; constantly growing, it reflects the work of the Craftsmen in residence. Moreover in 1990, the huge attic space above the gallery was insulated and converted into a studio to accommodate painting residencies.

The craft residencies at Grizedale are designed to give "makers" opportunities to develop their work in wood-related crafts. The only "brief" is to spend the time developing work in the most creative and productive way. It follows, that, with integrity, what is best for the Craftsman is often best for Grizedale.

In their location and structure these residencies are unique. The craftsmen have complete freedom to concentrate on the creative process offered by the residency.

At Grizedale, the craftsman's public consists of a wide spectrum of visitors, who come here to walk, ride, and linger, in all weathers. This audience is non-selected, and often "innocent" of the visual arts. The craftsman will decide for himself how he views his relationship with this public. All that is asked is that he communicates openly with them at a time to suit himself. The craftsman has a twenty-four hour access to the workshop throughout his stay, and keeps all the work produced, except certain pieces negotiably retained for the Grizedale collection.

Released from the constraints of working to a gallery deadline, or the selling limitations of their work, and placed within the freedom of this unique working situation, the various craftsmen have responded with courage, taken chances.

The Grizedale residencies have covered a wide range of wood-related crafts. In particular, support has been given to the woodturners. In 1986 the state of the craft was described by Jim Partridge in "Craft" magazine as "dull, gutless, lacking spirit and intellect, purposeless and valueless. With aspirations not going beyond making knick-knacks for suburban mantelpieces and endangering the dangerously addictive and mind-numbing habits of fancy techniques and tool fetishism". Ten years later, and with an established following of 30,000 amateur wood turners in Britain, this still no doubt is true.

However, there has been a revolution in the craft. The reverberations of the innovative and highly creative woodturning being produced in the United States motivated and inspired a new generation of British turners. In 1990 the Grizedale Society and Northern Arts, in support of this movement in Britain, awarded a twelve-month residency to Merryll Saylan, a woodturner from California. During the residency she travelled extensively on "her mission". She was actively involved with the Association of Woodturners of Great Britain, then in its infancy. With much local support, she inaugurated the Cumbrian Woodturners Association.

Since then, the British movement has matured, evolved, and "come of age", and residencies have been given to some of its best exponents. During 1994 Hayley Smith explored sculptural "constructivist" forms. She turned discs and shallow vessels of polished wood, incised lines, and inlayed metal and silver wire. These forms work in precise harmony, holding in them a pure, spiritual, timeless quality.

*Woodtuning: Mike Scott*

*Woodcarving: Wendy Brown*

*Peter Lloyd, boxmaker*

*Riven seat*
*Nigel Worlidge*

*Seats in the forest*

*Right: Nigel Ross*
*Below: Will Glanfield*
*Opposite, top: Nigel Ross*
*Below, left: Will Glanfield*
*Below, right: Nigel Ross*

Tim Stoke's residency produced a wealth of constructed, highly finished, dramatic turned forms, many in blackened wood and gold leaf. The ceremonial artifacts of an ancient court, or one to come?

Mike Scott came to work on his very distinctive "ancient" burred oak and elm vessels, turning, burning, hollowing and sandblasting them into submission. Evoking the magic of the woods outside the confines of the workshop. Mike also claimed that some of the sculpture at Grizedale had influenced him. His work, formal, controlled, contains secret hidden places, protected with hard geometric exterior forms.

Jurgen Ludwig, from East Germany, made joyful small turned forms specific to the Grizedale woods. His small intricate land-forms and interpretations of "tree-grown" geography, discovering inside his carefully selected "Grizedale Wood", caves, fells, valleys and water courses.

The Ulrike Scriba residency (with financial support from the Goethe Institute and Northern Arts) produced innovative work in Marquetry. She found at Grizedale the inspiration she sought and a quiet sanctuary. She states "my steps are slowly, like the tradition I work with. It demands sensitivity for the microscopic characteristic of wood. Precision from the beginning to the completion of one piece. This place protects and shows me where I come from. Let me find different and new ways". The intricacy of the non-figurative surface pattern covering her subtly constructed "Tower Box" and on her large, undulating trays (now in the Grizedale Collection) are fine examples of this craft in the late twentieth century.

Wendy Brown's residency in wood-carving produced two large, ambitious, carved panels on animal themes. Peter Lloyd constructed a variety of his strong, original boxes.

The residencies in furniture-making have contrasted greatly. Jonathon Stockton, who had the initial craft residency in 1988, confidently relocated his workshop to Grizedale, and carried on his highly productive skilled work using well-seasoned local timber. His designs echoed shapes from the late eighteenth century.

Allan Towse carefully constructed furniture also relating to an earlier period.

Nigel Worlidge, in 1994, selected a one hundred and forty year-old sessile oak from Grizedale, that had lain on the hillside for three years. His object was to explore the basic structure of the tree. He "rived" it along its grain. This produced the natural shapes and twisted baulks of green oak that inspired his furniture. Powerful, beautiful wood, sensitively yet strongly coming together into functional forms. The understanding respect for the character of the timber echoed the philosophy of John Makepeace, Nigel's former teacher. Truly furniture from this forest.

A fine stained-glass window was commissioned from Julian Stocks in 1992, and is located at the top of the staircase inside the Theatre-in-the Forest. The design is based on the topographical profile of Lake Windermere. Abstract ideas are taken from the music of John Cage and Eric Satie. The whole effect is one of tranquil reflection, reinforced through the use of blues and restful greens.

The Grizedale Society also plays an active role in the support of Crafts in Cumbria. Cumbria Craft Guild was started in 1988 to promote contemporary craft work of excellence in the country. Its annual exhibition is held during October in the Gallery in the Forest. Its president is Bill Grant.

In 1990 The Grizedale Society was the overall winner of the Prudential Award for the Arts, and received £ 100,000 in prize money. This enabled a new sculpture trail to be created, winding through Ridding Wood. It was designed to offer those members of the public, who through disability or age do not have access to the long-distance "Silurian Way" sculpture trail.

So that this trail could be enjoyed at leisure in maximum comfort, adequate seating needed to be an integral part of its design. This has been resolved in various ways. The essential criteria is the function of the seat, accessibility and comfort, also its relationshnip with the environment and the concept of the trail as a whole.

There are three seats by Jim Partridge and Liz Walmsley "The Serpentine Seat" is a Jim Partridge classic. Near the start of the trail, it invites one to rest before one begins. Constructed from a single beautiful S-shaped piece of oak, it still seems to be alive! It has an ancient presence, sited under a low-leaf beech canopy, one could imagine it had been there for generations.

The second seat "Sessile Seat" has the same qualities, but this is more the "expected" seat found along any path. Again, using one huge piece of sessile oak, its supporting legs are forever planted, immovable and strong. A seat where to watch "passers-by".

Their third seat is "The Sheltered Seat" which dominates a high bend in the trail near a ravine, with a wide dramatic view of the valley. A great turf covered "shelf" thrusts out from the hillside to form a wide roof, large enough to shelter twelve or more people beneath. Somehow, one is reminded of a ship and its deck. Minimal effective seating is interlocked into this wooden wall. Dynamic yet calm, functional and simple. The whole structure retains the integrity of its open windy site, yet creates a social meeting place to stop at and regroup.

Nigel Ross has three seats along the trail. His first is at the beginning of the trail, and relates to the form and scale of the Partridge/Walmsley entrance arch.   this seat commemorates John Mackie, erstwhile Chairman of the Forestry Commission and a true friend of Grizedale. A huge slab of oak is contained within an elegant curve of a root/branch-like form. It grows out of the ground in a curve that forms an arm which protectively sweeps over ones head. This seat creates its own environment, yet echoes the thick-branched rhodedendrons around it. A place to sit, meet and wait, it is visible from far down the trail.

Nigel's "lone seat" is an uncomfortable throne, a chair carved from one piece of wood. It is a statement of isolation and inaccessibility? Is it to emphasise the impossibility of access or a challenge to a disability? It is certainly not a place to rest, and has a sad quality about it.

His third "The Dunkeld Seat" is situated at the very far end of the trail. This is a splendid seat, a giant, situated in the finest location along the whole trail, commanding broad views across the valley to the forest beyond. Worked from one piece of Dunkeld Larch, sawn along its length, then cut in half and subtly joined again to give movement. It is contoured and sculptured to "tame" it. A great wild, yet placid creature, it somewhere has reference to wings and flight, on this wide open site.

One comes upon Will Glanfield's "Pacus" as one would find a seat in an Elizabethan garden carved with beetles taken from an old sampler. This altar-like seat is substantial in its drystone wall recess. However, on a trail designed for the disabled, the one foot-high stone step up to it is a major problem, and deterrent. As a seat it does not function, as an artefact along the way it is pleasant enough.

Will's "Three Kings" evokes ancient woodland tales. It is a large, "Royal" seat. Three seats in one, for three kings of the oak. He has used the oak leaf motif for the back-rests of each seat, and large carved acorns provide the feet.    Although the seat inhabits the Tolkien-like fairy world,  it retains its integrity and function, and does not appear Disney-like. It is sited immediately beneath a large, mature oak, on the "home stretch" of the trail. In this location it works well, strong yet peaceful.

The Ridding Wood Trail should be taken slowly and enjoyed. The aesthetics and utility of these seats making this a most pleasing and satisfying walk.

24

# PAINTING

## Vicky Slowe

The Lake District is a world heritage site in the consciousness of the English-speaking peoples if not in statute. Its image as a cultural icon has been fashioned over the last three hundred years thanks to the achievements of a plethora of painters, poets, prophets and pundits who came and saw and found inspiration.

The spiritual descendants of these artists and authors still come and see and find inspiration, still take nature as their guide through a wild work of art, but now carry with them an excess of cultural baggage, originating here in the cradle of landscape appreciation.

The residencies at Grizedale fulfil a strategic role in extending that genesis by encouraging exciting and radical artistic innovation.This not only enriches the experience of all those who view the resultant works of art and develops the creativity of the artists, but also stimulates debate about the place of art and the artist in the landscape, and about the importance of art in our lives.We must not forget that all good artists do - or at least attempt - the same thing: they help us to learn about ourselves.

In order to tell us who we are, art has to engage our minds and emotions, but sadly, as Brian Eno remarked when presenting the 1995 Turner Prize, "the intellectual climate surrounding the arts" currently lacks any "comprehensible public discussion about what art does for us, what is being learned from it, what it might enable us to do or think or feel that we couldn't before.  The making of new culture, which we do so well in England, is just about our only growth industry aside from heritage, cream teas, and land mines, but the lack of a clear connection between all that creative activity and the mental life of the rest of society leaves the whole project poorly understood, poorly supported and poorly exploited."[1]

Such remarks underline the paramount importance of the arts experience at Grizedale. Visitors exploring the forest trails on foot or mountain-bike have chance encounters with non-intrusive sculptures which emerge subtly from their natural surroundings and then fade back into the environment. Such an experience is integral and natural; the works "belong" insitu, to all who have the eyes and hearts to see them. Those with a mind to do so can buy a guide map, and seek out more, against the dramatic backcloth of a large working forest.

Another approach to "more" is provided by The Gallery in the Forest, a deliberately non-threatening, low-key exhibition space, converted from a former saw mill, which sits naturally in its setting. Working drawings, models (or maquettes) for sculptures, photographs of the more ephemeral, fragile works, are displayed non-confrontationally, for the enjoyment of those unable to tackle - through age or infirmity - the rigours of the forest tracks, and to whet the appetites of those wondering in which direction to explore.

*Carol Tyler at work in the Painting Studio*     *Meg Falconer, artist*

An internal window allows visitors to look through into the wood-turning workshop where the fortunate can see skilled craftsmen at work. An external staircase leads to the Painting Studio, a well-lit attic space above the Gallery, which provides a base for current painter-in-residence. Both painters and craftsmen are encouraged to welcome visitors to their studios in an attempt to break down the barriers between the artist and the public, and to establish the dialogue and debate identified as so rewarding by Brian Eno, and to promote sales.

Exhibitions of work produced during craft and painting residencies are held regularly in the Gallery in the Forest, and representative examples of the work of past residencies are displayed in the Gallery and in the entrance foyer and stairway of The Theatre in the Forest, itself an integral part of the holistic arts experience at Grizedale.

Work shown in the Gallery in the Forest is always indigenous to Grizedale, with the one exception of the annual exhibition of the Cumbria Craft Guild each autumn.

The central purpose, the mission, of the painting residencies at Grizedale is to bring an artist to live and work in a small rural community in the heart of a large production forest, and to give that artist a respite from the mundane pressures of everyday life, a breathing space in which to respond to a new environment and take a fresh direction. The residency is a gift of time and opportunity to explore immediate reactions and experiment with novel approaches, to think about meanings, and to drink up the charged atmosphere of a place resonant with cultural and environmental overtones and undertones.

Grizedale epitomises the paradox that is the Lake District; a natural skeleton shaped by the elements but clothed by the managing hand of man. Indeed, the whole land mass of the British Isles below 3,5000 ft. has been managed by man for at least three thousand years. Management styles have evolved over that time-span, as have human perceptions of place, landscape, religion and the scheme of things. What Abraham Lincoln so imaginatively described as "the mystic chimes of memory" ring loudly throughout the Lake District, resounding particularly strongly over the moorland now clothed by Grizedale forest, where the boy Wordsworth, a pupil at Hawkshead Grammar School roamed and trapped woodcock; where the young Turner caught his breath at the sublime grandeur of the Coniston Fells; where the seer Ruskin observed the pollutant effects of industry on cloud and sunset, prophesying the green-house effect and global warning; where the exhausted one-time radical portrait-painter, Romney, hoped for peaceful retirement; where Tennyson honey-mooned... Many famous feet have walked upon these particular mountains green, and the footsteps still echo down the years.

Neolithic man, his Bronze-Age descendants, the celts, the Romans, the Norsemen, Norman forester-monks, Elizabethan iron-smelting entrepeneurs, George Fox and the Quakers, Wesley, Victorian ship-builders and ocean-line owners, Beatrix Potter and Authur Ransome have all known this patch of land.

Add to that the fact that "Grizedale" is now short-hand for a forest: peripheral fragments of the ancient oak wildwood of the Furness fells, disordered and coherent, flank large tracts of ordered conifers, harvested and re-planted in tidy blocks, whilst some decorative planting of ornamental, specimen trees in the Grizedale valley enhances its picturesque qualities. The word "forest" carries many connotations.

As the journalist Jill Parkin has perceptively commented, "somewhere in our English psyche lurks a wood where anything can happen. It's where Robin Hood and Maid Marian wander, or it's the Forest of Arden, depending on your literary learnings. Whichever you choose, it's an outlaw alternative to the city and order".[2]

That is the crux of the attraction of Grizedale for visitors and artists alike.

The painters Tiana Marie, Tony Smith, Phil Duthie, Fiona Adams and Meg Falconer, have each responded - though differently - to the Romantic refrain so strongly heard at Grizedale. Tiana Marie's tanglewood thickets are the Sleeping Beauty's defence. Tony Smith's Greenwood Glades set the scene for adventure, whilst Fiona Adam's idyllic woods are ripe for rustic revels. Meg Falconer worked on four large panels which told the ancient tale of "Sir Gawain and the Green Knight", (The battle between Summer and Winter), exploring the essential continued fertility of the land, seasonal rhythms, the interconnection of all life, through the allegories of ancient celtic myth and Arthurian legend. Two months at Grizedale, in the early summer of 1995, extended this painter's vocabulary of signs, symbols and new images to rich and magical effect.

Iain Robertson and Clare Wardman entitled the exhibition at the close of their 1993 residencies, "Back to the Sun", implying not only their return to nature as inspiration but also their re-orientation to the Norse world, which defines North as the direction one faces with one's back to the sun at noon. Such direction - to the work of recent abstract painters in Northern Europe is implicit in the rejection of obviously elegant and sophisticated techniques and explicit in the celebration of the primitive, organic and direct qualities of the act of painting. Their work is full of the energy of life, is rigorously aggressive, rough and raw in texture, with the paint scraped, scumbled and hewn, to evoke mood and feelings of change in a totally non-representational manner. Both are city painters : Grizedale influenced their forms (softer, rounder, more eroded, less structured, more fluid and spacious) and palettes (earth, leaf and sky tones). As Andrew Patrizio of Glasgow Museums has noted, "their paintings reward repeated study and always offer enjoyment long after first contact. They have the ability to snarl the eye, to trap it as if walking through gorse and bracken. The effort and the challenge is ten-fold more exciting than purveying a manicured lawn".[3]

Carol Tyler came to Grizedale in the late summer of 1995 with the expressed aim of developing and extending an already existing process based on her experience of place - the light and atmosphere, the shapes and materials - rather than of producing "finished" work. She became fascinated by the fates befalling the forest trees, watching them harvested by the foresters, seeing them toppled by the wind, observing them slowly bleaching and decaying through time.   In her earlier Grizedale picture, the activity of writing a "long list of often quite violent descriptive verbs"[4] becomes her "drawing", and prints and rubbings from a found log become the main motif. Toward the end of her residency, the u-shape of the glacial Grizedale valley became a prominent feature of her work.

A native of Wigan, Peter Clayton, who was in residence in the autumn of 1995, has long sought inspiration in the wilder corners of Britain. He found that working and living on the spot afforded him a greater intimacy with the landscape; he was able to observe every subtle change in light and mood, and grew progressively more intensely aware of Grizedale's underlying strength and complexity, claiming that he began to feel part of the landscape rather than a mere observer.[5] He drew and painted outdoors - generally in good weather - depicting transitory, fleeting moods and light effects down the Grizedale valley or over coniston Old Man or Wetherlam. Direct contact with the elements strengthened his work; his truncated images and compositions grew bolder, less fussy and contrived, and his colours more vibrant as he began to trust his eyes rather than his preconceptions, and to paint the unbelievably brilliant azure of the Lakeland sky during an Indian Summer, andto realise the truth of Ruskin's dictum that "sunlighted grass is yellow".[6]

Joanna Hart and Phil Duthie were also captivated by the true rather than the preconceived colours of the forest, expressing them in abstract shafts of light percolating through the leaf canopy to light and shade the forest floor. Adams was interested in pools of light, Duthie in shafts and columns.

Over the autumn, winter and early spring of 1993/94, Alasdair Urquhart responded to Grizedale with a series of heroic impressions of the working forest where man, horse and machine pit their strengths against the elements to harvest timber.

To quote Kenneth Clark (discussing John Constable), "I am reminded that Wordsworth, in his Preface of 1802, says that he chose rustic subjects because in them the passions of men are incorporated with the beautiful and permanent forms of nature! "[7]

Some two hundred years on - and not a million light years distant from the pantheistic poet's alma mater at Hawkshead Grammar school - that still holds good.

Urquhart's vivid paintings and pastels express the spirit of the place through the immediacy, the shock of recognition that springs from painting en plein air. The characterful portraits of the working foresters, whom he came to know and admire for their inherent knowledge, skills and lore, demonstrate his empathy with, and innate perception of true countryman's sense of comfortable ease with the natural world.

Life and growth infuse his pictures through the expression of movement, light and colour, invoking a hymn of praise for the incredible, wonderful joy of being alive. Pulses are quckened through spontaneous dashes of astringent lemons and limes as sunlight filters through fragile spring leaves; spirits are raised via deft touches of brash salmon pink, reeking of resinous turpentine, and vibrating against the soft indigos and violets of the dim shadows under the spruce. The painterly qualities are seductively obvious.

At Grizedale, Urquhart's approach to figurative subjects gained an epic quality, and his palette a vibrancy, which can only enhance his reputation as one of Britain's most exciting contemporary representational painters.

Panaylotis Kalorkoti's work seems simple at first glance, because of his use of simplified almost hieroglyphic forms and basic textures and restrained (but very sophisticated) tones. His child-like glee at successfully hi-jacking symbols and images created by others and then incorporating them into his own acrylics and

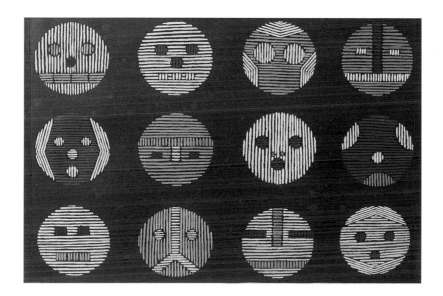

*Panayiotis Kalorkoti from* **Reflections on Grizedale** *(acrylic on paper)*

multi-plate etchings is palpable. It is evident that he enjoys the visual pun (and basic truth) on juxtaposing his portrait of Grizedale's inspiration, Bill Grant, with a view of David Kemp's The Ancient Forester and a shot of the same sculptor's maquette, Deer Hunter, in his multi-plate etching Grizedale 1.

This etching is the key to Kalorkoti's response to the complexity that is Grizedale. Other elements in this composition include Steven Darbishire's neo-Romantic logo for The Grizedale Society, designed in 1969, and featuring trees, deer, squirrel, and Pan/Pied Piper; Robert Koenig's phallic growth symbol, the sign post, and catapult - like Triangular Suspension, and plotting watchers; block-like books entitled Churchill Fellowship, Theatre in the Forest, Grizedale, Sculpture and Grizedale forest, (the bricks from which the Grizedale Arts Experience has been built); a wooden desk and an obviously paper support for the image, (wood products derived from forests).

Grizedale 1 is thus clearly a visual metaphor representing the cultural paradox that is Grizedale : commercial forest, Romantic wildwood, nature reserve, wildlife habitat, shoot, hunting country, footpath, cycleway, adventure playground centre for the performing arts, outdoor gallery of contemporary art...

Kalorkoti's intention[8] is to make us question what we see, query whether we see what we think we see. He explores such paradoxes with fun and humour, forcing us to shift our attention from sculptured deer to live ones, from wooden webs to real gossamer, from human creation to the divine. He also prompts us into noticing that the figurative sculptures are much more visible than the abstract ones, (many of which are much more ambitious in scale, but which tend to melt into the camouflage of their surroundings), thus making us examine what is natural and what is man-made, and so contemplate the "pathetic fallacy": the ambiguity of mankind's place in the scheme of things. For, if humans are part of the natural world, how is it possible to differentiate the man-made from the naturally formed?

According to the writer and critic John Berger:

"The notion that art is the mirror of nature is one that only appeals in periods of scepticism. Art does not imitate nature, it imitates a creation, sometimes to propose an alternative world, sometimes simply to amplify, to confirm, to make social the brief hope offered by nature. Art is an organised response to what nature allows us to glimpse occasionally. Art sets out to transform the potential recognition into an unceasing one. It proclaims man in the hope of receiving a surer reply ... the transcendental face of art is always a form of prayer".[9]

These comments shed light on the responses to Grizedale vouchsafed not only by the artists and public in general but also by Kalorkoti in particular.

Generally speaking, whereas the sculptors in residence use the found materials immediately to hand at their chosen site - wood, slate, earth, water, abandoned scrap and industrial relics - the painters tend to explore fresh methods and techniques for using their traditional paints to express the growth, decay, light, movement, translucency, hardness, heaviness, and natural rhythm of the seasons, which are integral to the forest, and both implicit and explicit in the site-specific sculpture.

Sally Matthews has experimented with mud and muck - and a few pine needles - to draw her bristling wild boar and snarling wolves.

Andy Goldsworthy has "painted" brilliant - if ephemeral - abstract compositions using torn autumnal leaves and the scarlet stalks of sycamore, and has taken not just a wall but a trail of bracken fronds for a walk which follows the sure, delicate line of an Old Master - or Paul Klee. Janet Ledsham has combined ethereal felts with skeleton leaves from the forest floor to create wonderfully evocative flowing garments for the denizens of an enchanted wildwood, and Jackie Scammell has squeezed and moulded and tinted and dyed wood pulp into "paper paintings" which capture the silence, the contemplative twilight, the broodiness, and the essential growth of Grizedale.

The sculptures at Grizedale rely, for the power of their impact, on the projection of nature's transitory effects on their "permanence", including their gradual decay back into the earth of which they were formed. The sculptures are in essence, temporary, in memento mori : like man, they have a finite span.

But the paintings stand for immortality. Their purpose is to capture, to freeze-frame, in perpetuity, magic moments of perception. So we reach yet another paradox.

John Berger is categoric that "all the languages of art have been developed as an attempt to transform the instantaneous into the permanent".[10]

In the light of the arts experience at Grizedale, construe.

And develop a much-needed debate.

The truth - or the truths - are out there.

## REFERENCES

1.   Speech at the Tate Gallery, as reported in the Daily Telegraph, 6th January 1996.

2.   Jill Parkin, "Let nature look after itself", Weekend Telegraph, 20th. January 1996.

3.   Andrew Patrizio, introduction to exhibition catalogue, "Back to the sun", Gallery in the Forest, 1993.

4.   Artist's statement

5.   Artist's statement

6.   John Ruskin "On First Practice", The Elements of Drawing, first published in 1857 by Smith, Elder & Co. London; illustrated edition with notes by Bernard Dunstan published 1991 by the Herbert Press Limited, London.

7.   Kenneth Clark, Looking at Pictures, "Constable : Study for the Leaping Horse", published by John Murray, London 1960.

8.   For a fuller discussion and appreciation see Edward Lucie-Smith's Text in Panayiotis Kalorkoti: "Reflections of Grizedale", (Acrylics, watercolours, Etchings),  The Grizedale Society, 1995.

9.   John Berger, The White Bird, Chatto and Windus, 1985, (known also as the Sense of Sight, Pantheon Books, Random House inc).

10. Ibid.

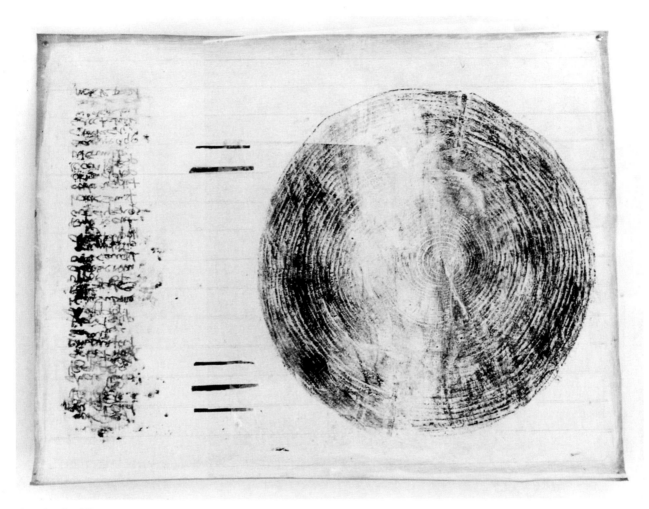

*Carol Tyler* **Thesaurus**

# SCULPTURE

## DAVID KEMP

Every year, for the last twenty years, sculptors have been coming to Grizedale to spend time living and working in the forest. From faltering beginnings, the sculpture project, like the forest, has undergone the processes of growth, atrophy, regeneration and change. Sculptors have come to work in Grizedale from a variety of urban and rural backgrounds, from Britain and abroad: Holland, New Zealand, America, Bulgaria, Japan, France and the former Yugoslavia. In return, many British sculptors have been invited, as a consequence of their experience at Grizedale, to work abroad and on other outdoor sculpture projects in Britain.

The success of the sculpture project at Grizedale is renowned. It has gained a national and international reputation which is reflected by the numerous applications to work or visit received from all over the world, and by the many new sculpture trails which have sprung up over the last few years. The Grizedale project has become an institution and the forest sculptures a major visitor attraction. Over the years nearly two hundred sculptures have been built in the forest. Although many of these sculptures survive, Grizedale is not, and has never been, a sculpture park.

The forest sculpture project was originally devised as a three to six month residency for young artists. Basic living accommodation was provided, and the sculptors were given the opportunity to live and work within a working forest and its local community.

For most of the sculptors this was a very different experience from that gained by their established practices. There has rarely been a workshop or studio provided for sculpture at Grizedale. Instead, the facilities of college or studio are exchanged for the huge solitude of the woods. The sculptors are left to their own resources, the forest becomes workshop, inspiration, and the source of a vast array of raw materials. There is Room to Lumber.

The first sculptors working at Grizedale had the woods to themselves, there were no precedents to follow or ignore. There was, and still is, a school of opinion that felt that trees were preferable to sculpture, and that the point of view established by sculpture in a woodland setting merely spoiled the view. The first sculpture sited in the forest was, by its uniqueness, unnaturally conspicuous. Ironically the simple elegance of some of these early works has ensured their survival for nearly twenty years. As more and more sculptures were made and sited in the forest, many precedents have been established over siting and use of materials. The sculptors have learned from each other's successes and failures, yet continued to find individual responses to the challenge of building sculpture in the forest.

Work created out of doors gives rise to a whole set of practical and logistical problems not encountered in studio based work. Theory is often modified by working practices, The possibilities inherent in building large scale outdoor work, off the beaten track, have created a steep learning curve for many artists, who have had to find or invent new ways of working, moving, lifting, building, and siting their work.

Many of the forest sculptures were built directly on site. This practice might be regarded as a particular characteristic of Grizedale sculpture, a subtly different procedure from many other sculpture parks or trails. At Grizedale the sculptor has the opportunity to choose a site amongst 9,000 acres of trees and 75 miles of forest tracks. For most artists the site was much more than a backdrop. The sculpture was built right there in the woods, designed to respond to aspects of the chosen site. A dialogue has been created between the sculpture and its immediate environment, which might be regarded as a component of the piece. Some artists have been reluctant to place their work conspicuously, seeking hidden and neutral spaces and finding enclosed areas that would be "activated" by their sculptures. Other artists have chosen more obvious sites, some already possessing a strong indigenous character.

Working out of doors often means getting wet. Every day spent in the forest can be different, depending on the weather and the season. For a sculptor working alone in the forest, it is difficult to remain unaffected by its many moods and changes: shafts of sunlight filtered through the trees; the rumble of thunder from the mountains; rain in infinite and subtle variety from drips to drizzle, hail and cloudbursts, drifting clouds of soft, enveloping mist; snow mirrored in the black tarn, falling upwards towards itself; the green dance of the larch in spring. Sculptors will have their own first hand experiences and memories of working in the forest. Alone, and working quietly, or sitting and watching, one becomes aware of the sounds of the forest and of its other denizens. The gurgling of the beck, the sighing of the trees in the wind, the roar of distant chain saws, the cough of the red deer, the mew of a buzzard above the forest canopy, the hoot of an owl, the squeak of a vole, the rustling of bushes, the snap of a twig that breaks the silence.

The forest provides a large range of raw materials, principally wood and stone. The artists have used these in a diverse and inventive number of ways. Some work has been created very simply, using found materials assembled by hand, whilst others have been made deliberately with materials and technology that contrast with their surroundings.

Trees are obviously the major forest resource, providing a variety of products. Heavy timber is sawn into blocks, planks, baulks, battens or laths. It can also be carved, cut or shaped with hand tools or chain saw. Woods from different trees have a range of characteristics and qualities. The heart of the oak is much more durable than its sapwood. Soft woods don't last long out in the elements unless treated with preservatives (often toxic to other life forms). The mighty beech, with its huge limbs, is useless for outdoor work, as it succumbs to fungal attack within a few years of cutting. The resin in the European Larch makes it light but durable. Some artists have used the natural shapes inherent in tree growth to make their sculpture, choosing windblown and unhewn timber. Others have used branches, poles, willow withies and bark. Some artists have worked with living trees, or planted them as part of their sculptures.

Stone, in the form of Silurian slate, is also readily available in the forest. This kind of stone splits easily into strata, and has been used extensively for dry stone walling throughout the locality. Sculptors have cut it, carved it, drilled it, pinned it and stacked it, borrowing a number of local walling techniques. Other local stone has been used in a variety of ways.

One is never far from water in the forest, standing in tarns and pools and running in becks. Water has been used as an essential component of some sculptures.

Other materials, such as earth, turf, peat and mud have found applications in forest sculpture, as well as cement, glass and a variety of found objects. Curiously steel is not greatly in evidence. Although it must be considered as an essential shaper of the forest, in the form of the spade, irrigation shovel, saw and axe, few sculptors have used it in their work, except for fixings and fittings

The forest itself is in a continuous state of change. It is a tree farm, and quite large areas are subject to thinning and felling. Harvesting can lay bare large sections of hillside and open up sudden new vistas. These areas are usually replanted immediately after clearing, and the fast growing modern hybrid conifers rapidly fill the new spaces. Forest fires and storms have also caused sudden and unexpected change.

The areas surrounding many of the older sculptures have radically altered over the years. Work hidden amongst mature trees has been exposed, whilst other sculptures sited in open clearings have become obscured by new growth.

The sculptures are subject to the same natural cycles of change that rule the rest of the forest and its wildlife: the moss grows, the wood rots, the sculptures are mostly biodegradable and eventually return to earth. Sculptures that have started to disintegrate are removed annually. Permanency is only a relative term in a forest setting. There are degrees of endurance. Even the stone, the bedrock of the forest, which four hundred and fifty million years ago formed the floor of the Silurian Sea, is still in a state of change. The mountain ridges rip open the soft underbellies of the clouds sweeping in from the sea, the rain courses down the hillsides, slowly eroding the rocks. The clouds are eating mountains.

Grizedale provides a diversity of spaces and places to work in. The open vistas of wooded hillside, the saw toothed coniferous ridges, and the secret spaces between trees provide more than a background. The forest is the matrix in which the sculpture is set. It is difficult to consider the work without reflecting on its relationship with the immediate environment, the "natural" world of stone and wood and sky.

Paths into "nature" have been well trodden in Britain by artists from Turner to Richard Long. Art has long imitated nature and represented it as an ideal, or an escape from life's vicissitudes. From classical Arcadias to recent renewals of Taoism, the "natural" environment has been perceived as both mirror and contrast to the human domain. More recently nature has been described as culture's horizon. Our attitudes to the "great outdoors" have, like our countryside, undergone processes of continuing change. It is only twice the life span of an oak tree that separates us from a Europe where true wildernesses existed. Nature and its wild things were a threat to life and limb, people built walls and fences to keep them at bay. Within the life span of a single oak tree society had begun to assume attitudes of superiority over nature, and ideas about "landscape" began to emerge. Now, at the end of the second millennium, there are few wildernesses left in Britain, except those between our ears. The fences and walls are going up again, this time to protect what is left of nature from our ravages. People are campaigning to save trees from bulldozers.

The landscape at Grizedale has been through most of these stages. At the visitor centre a development is traced from the valley of pigs to pig iron, from private park land to government tree farm, nature reserve and, currently, forest park.

Within this last incarnation the forest has become a recreational resource, serving diverse and sometimes conflicting needs. Although still a working forest, it is also an outdoor classroom, where people can experience nature for themselves. Educational facilities and the inevitable merchandising opportunities co-exist at the visitors' centre. There is a variety of forest and nature trails open to the public, where woodlands can be explored on foot, wheelchair or mountain bike. Nature as recreation encompasses not only the opportunity to see red deer in a wild habitat, or to stand transfixed by the beauty of a beech tree, but also the teeth gritting, tyre slipping, tree splitting, pitting of man and machine against nature, as experienced annually, when the Lombard Rally races through the forest.

The cutting edge of modern technologies is also represented by the giant machines currently harvesting timber resources within Grizedale. These great tree eaters have made redundant much of the local workforce, traditionally employed in the forest. Although the use of motor vehicles is strictly controlled within the forest itself, their use is drastically changing the shape of local communities. Extensive road building programmes combined with greatly increased private car ownership has created easy access to the countryside. Paradoxically the sheer volume of visitors seeking to commune with nature in the Lake District threatens to overwhelm the very qualities they seek.

Behind the freedom and diversity of the forest sculpture, there lies another creative and adaptable structure not immediately evident in the work itself. This is the administrative scheme set up by Bill Grant of the Grizedale Society and assisted through much of its development by Peter Davies, during his time as Visual Arts Officer for Northern Arts. Using the analogy of a tree, with the sculpture represented as the branches and leaves and all that is visible above ground, then the roots, a huge and largely invisible system of nourishment and support, have been established by Bill and Peter. This has been a difficult and demanding job, undertaken with perseverance, patience and humour. Their enthusiasm for the project has been equalled by their deep personal interest in sculpture and encouragement for the sculptors who have worked at Grizedale. Peter Davies has now left Northern Arts, but Bill Grant remained firmly in the saddle, continuing to provide the commitment and imagination required to sustain the sculpture project, and with a sharp eye out for new horizons and possibilities.

The Forestry Commission has been an essential partner in the project since it was incepted. The foresters have provided good natured and friendly advice as well as practical assistance to a generation of sculptors. The local community has also been an important influence. Sculptors have been working and living around Satterthwaite for nearly twenty years. They have brought their families, their friends and students to the place, making demands on the resources and facilities and crowding out the pub. Local people have taken a friendly interest in the sculpture, and have often formed strong opinions about the work in their forest. Working in the forest may often be a solitary business, but the woods are far from private. Work under progress is noticed by the locals and visitors, and sculptors may find themselves in receipt of unsolicited opinions and feedback about their work. This public aspect of Grizedale sculpture is another component informing the work, and making it very different from a college or studio environment.

As the project has grown, so has the audience. Works made in the solitude of the forest are now seen by a wide audience, some of whom may have come principally to view the sculptures. Groups of students arrive on day tours, arts administrators are whisked around the forest in vehicles to view specific works. Some people only see photographs and confuse this with the actual experience of forest sculpture. Removed from its environmental context, the significance of much of the work is impaired. The forest is reduced to the role of an outdoor art gallery.

The photographs in this book make some effort to explain the sculpture within the context of its environment, but there are no settings on any camera that can fully explain this changing relationship. The sculptors' statements offer an insight to their individual experiences and concerns, but these are only clues, not the whole picture.

The best way to experience Grizedale Forest sculpture is to put down this book, pull on your boots and get out in them woods. Within the soul calming rhythm of walking perceive that the eye, the foot and the brain travel together but do not always follow the same path. The trail into the forest leads up hill and down through the dreams of five million trees. Through the bobbing profusion of stone, wood, leaf and sky, the eye seeks for features. Sometimes it is a bird or deer, sometimes a root or branch, sometimes a sculpture. The sculptures are anonymous; the formality of the art gallery and its persistent interpretative panels are missing. The observers must make their own decisions. The sculpture is the prime communicator, requiring you to decide the nature of its dialogue with its surroundings. The pieces are brought in and out of focus by the passer by, they are intervals within a forest walk. Sculpture in the open air is much more than sticking statues in the rain. It has the potential to be an integrated response to specific environments and situations. Siting their work in public can lead artists to reconsider their own situation within society.

Most of the sculptors have come to work in Grizedale at the beginning of their careers. They have had the opportunity to experiment with ideas, techniques and themes which they may have been able to develop subsequently. Several established artists, who have already developed specialised techniques and concerns, have worked at Grizedale, finding unique opportunities to extend and put into practice new ideas. All the sculptors have had the opportunity to discover their own interface with the forest and pursue their own courses. The range of sculptures produced illustrates a great diversity in theme, content and approach. It is this variety that makes Grizedale unique. Although the forest has become a workshop for so many sculptors, there is no recognisable "Grizedale School" of sculpture. A whole generation of sculptors has grown up since the start of the project. Continuing changes in social conditions and environmental concerns seem likely to inform and modify the agendas of the young sculptors who will soon be seeking to discover and express their own reactions to the "natural landscape". Hopefully Grizedale will continue to be a catalyst for new and thoughtful work.

# Sculpture Spotters Guide

Sculptures appear and vanish with each new season. The sculpture map is renewed at regular intervals and is a useful guide, but there are no footnotes by the footpath and sculpture spotters might find the following suggestions useful when tracking down forest sculpture

1. Keep a sharp look-out. Is it a bird, a beast, a stump, a root or a sculpture? Some sculptures, like other forest denizens, are well camouflaged, and sometimes hidden off the beaten track

2. Be attentive on approach. The work may be designed to change with aspect. It may look different when viewed from a distance than when seen close up. Walk around the sculpture, there may be other features on the other side, The work might be serial, with other elements in the vicinity.

3. Be careful. Although the work is maintained and removed when it begins to lose its integrity, sculpture, often made from forest materials, is eventually subject to change, rot and decay.

4. Be curious. There are a number of questions that might be considered:

    What has the sculpture been made from? Why have these particular materials been chosen, where did they come from, are they integral to the sculpture, or might another choice of material been more effective or appropriate?

    How was the sculpture put together, and how does it stand up? What sort of technology has been used to make the sculpture? Are things cut, carved, jointed, pinned, bolted, nailed, glued, woven, bent, tied, stacked, or balanced together?

    Why is it here? Why has the sculptor sited the work in this place? How does it relate to its immediate environment? Does it fit in, is it secret or conspicuous? What elements are there in the vicinity that may have determined the sculptor's choice? How has it changed with the seasons, and how have its surroundings changed since it was made?

    What is it about? This is the biggest question of all. Some references may be more obvious than others, and the list is endless: The forest, growth, atrophy, change, rhythm, animal and plant life, local crafts and defunct industries, different kinds of space, time, distance, the earth, the sky? There may be no words to describe the feelings and ideas inherent in an individual piece of work. Ultimately sculpture is in itself a language, some pieces are simple, some more complex or paradoxical. Although the sculptor's statements can offer some illumination, the sculptures themselves should be regarded as eloquent, and to be speaking for themselves.

    David Kemp, St. Just, West Cornwall, February 1996

*David Kemp has worked at Grizedale in 1982, 1987 and 1995. He has built a variety of large public sculptures in both rural and urban settings. He works full time as a sculptor and continues to develop his work within the context of the post-industrial landscape around his home in West Cornwall.*

40

# WALTER BAILEY

### Cloak of Seasons
#### 1995

Whatever faith or belief we carry, the tides of nature move around and through us. Every breath we take is an affirmation of our connection with the earth. In the "Cloak of Seasons" the figure wears a constantly changing garment of earth and sky. I celebrate the cloak we all share.

42

## ANNA BEST

### The Map
#### 1991

Project to cast and invert a hill. Inversion landscape : mountain / lake..forest clearing: demolition site... hill: elevation, island, plateau... ground: surface, earth/sky boundary... survey: traverse, path, curve...

|  |  |
|---|---|
| *cast* | *invert* |
| *process* | *transform* |
| *cover* | *dismantle* |
| *layer* | *remove* |
| *contact* | *confront* |
| *focus* | *structure* |
| *follow* | *join* |
| *remain* | *convolute* |
| *scrutinise* | *turn* |
| *repeat* | *elevate* |
| *fit* | *horizon* |
| *section* | *fragment* |
| *delineate* | *place* |

44

# KEES BIERMAN

## RAISED WALL
### 1992

Stone is predominant in the landscape of the Lake District. In the sculpture I have broken the direct relationship between Stone and Earth, by lifting up the dry-stone wall and putting it on a wooden construction, which can then be perceived both visually and physically at eye-level.

46

# JOHANNES BLUDAU

### Declining
### 1994

From the Oak's dead misshapen mass a new organic shape evolves, manifestly intrusive, weblike, in its challenge to Man and Nature.

# CHRIS BOOTH

## In Celebration of A Tor
### 1993

I feel I should be responding to the stone with stone, therefore to the earth and what shaped the surface here: ice.

Silurian slate was once silt in water, and with fossils was deposited then subjected to enormous metamorphic pressures to eventually form stone.

Technically I tip my hat to the people before, the stone walls they left. However I want to free myself (and the viewer) into a refreshing use of stone, and to create a sculptural form that openly celebrates a particular natural Tor that symbolises this Silurian land.

The sculpture is a mark, a celebratory organic mark that curves as it rises. Curves that are similar to the ice-sculpted Tor it celebrates, curves just like the surrounding ice-sculpted landscape and the trees growing on it (trees too are made of minerals from the land); curves like the original water waves that deposited the silt and the flow shapes of the ice age.

# CHARLES BRAY

### Light Column
#### 1995

This work is based on spectacular rock formations with vertical strata in the Gorges d'Allier in the Auvergne. Water had been running down in some places and when caught by the sunlight gave an illusion of the rock being split by strips of glass.

In Light Column, strips of glass have been fitted in various lengths so that the horizontal joints reflect the light to the vertical surfaces to give points of greater brilliance.

# RICHARD CAINK

### Habitat
#### 1994

"Habitat" is an installation which is fun and accessible, engaging the viewer both physically, by their presence, and intellectually. The intention as far as 'meaning' is concerned, is to articulate notions of our relationship to the natural world, taking the familiar trappings of a domestic living-room and placing them out of context, trying to relocate us within 'the forest' where our origins lie, or at least reminding us we are still embedded within the fabric of nature.

54

## IRAIDA CANO

### Between Elephants
Rock painting,1995

The largest and most powerful creature that walks this planet. The elephants appear, emerge, surrounding you, hide themselves in the hills, look at you very intensely.

# HILARY CARTMEL

## Her Insistent Stream
### 1985

Three months in the forest and it rained every day. The very wetness of the summer was wholly appropriate to what I wanted from Grizedale and that atmosphere I hope was permeated into the sculpture. My work at Grizedale could be loosley encapsulated under the title of "Women and Water". So Grizedale's streams and waterfalls as well as the torrential summer weather was perfect. I had a great deal of contact with the forest workers. Nine of the forest workers helped move my first sculpture onto its site down a ästeep bank and over a stream to one of the islands above Force Falls. The Huge oak trunk I carved into "Her Insistent Stream" was said to be only fit for fire wood, but it proved excellent for my purpose.

58

# JEREMY CUNNINGHAM

## Axe Life Cycle
### 1991

Through working in rural locations, I have become very aware of the variety of natural cycles which take place around me, and parallel cycles which result from various forms of husbandry. In the last year I have sought ways to use these cycles in my sculpture whilst continuing a long-running interest in the sculptural potential of hand tool forms..

In the "Axe Life Cycle" for the Grizedale forest, my concerns with cycles and tools have come together. I hope I have turned the usual associations of the axe literally on their head. The axe-head has a similar shape to the first leaves of some seedlings which are drawn out of the ground by elongation of the shoot.

**60**

# GEURT VAN DIJK

## Cathedral of Unknown Desires
### 1992

I count the days... started in the morning and the day finished with care and then sunslow; the contemplation, the navel staring! between the light and the dark; twilight, sunslow. One day as a thousand years. A "hommage" (dedication) to Kurt Schwitters; "Cathedral for the Unknown Desires"

About the intense desire of a small human being and the fear for eternity.

62

# ALAN FRANKLIN

### Harbour
**1995**

"Harbour" is an attempt to build a piece of work which is in empathy with its environment without being sentimental, romantic or backward looking, and which takes on both the scale and the natural beauty of the forest. Above all it should embody my personal approach to being.

64

# ANDY FROST

## Stag Herd Roof
### 1993

A disused building, now partially re-roofed, deer emerge from the forest, inquisitive and nervous.   They explore and inhabit the new space, standing staggered, (hence the title), still and alert - a futile attempt to blend into new surroundings.

Above: Adventure Playground

66

# ANDY GOLDSWORTHY

## Taking a Wall for a walk
### 1990

A dry stone wall is an expression of the stone used and the landscape through which it travels - over hills, along ridges, down gullys, around outcrops.... using the lie of the land to find a route.

Whichever direction the wall goes and however it is perceived, the structure remains a work of art. It is not bound by the practical demands required for agrarian purposes. Although making strong connections to the craft and tradition of walling, it essentially remains a work of nature and art.

68

# RICHARD HARRIS

### Quarry Structure
### 1977

The construction system used in "Quarry Structure" was originally conceived as a bridging device to follow the line of a stream. Unexpectedly I found the quarry site which immediately made sense of the idea. The quarry had been fenced off, overgrown and forgotten. The Structure, nosing out into the path, acts as a device to open up the space, both physically and visually.

70

# ANTONY HOLLOWAY

### Water Wheel
#### 1994

Water is an essential life giving element in nature's complex network of inter-related cycles. It is fitting that it should rotate the days, seasons and lives on the wheel. The wheel is like the relentlessly beating heart of a living forest.

72

# DAVID KEMP

### The Ancient Forester
#### 1995

"The Ancient Forester", a figure of great antiquity, lurks deep in the Gothic forests and wilderness between our ears. From Cernunnos, the horned Celtic deity to Tolkien's Tom Bombardil, he represents an idealised image of man the hunter, the mystic, the guardian. He lives in responsible husbandry with nature, and seeks a symbiotic relationship with his environment and its renewable resources.

Centrally-heated, carpeted, cocooned and double-glazed, we are becoming separate from our real life-support systems. Dazzled by the power of our clever machines, we are sawing off the branch we sit on. The Ancient Forester is a noble ideal. The wooden figure is huge joke. It didn't cost an arm and a leg to make - only an oak tree. Timber !

74

# BORIS KISHKILOV

## Merry-go-round
### 1991

The source of the artistic idea of my work is the traditional merry-go-round, which appears in the ancient Bulgarian folklore festival on Saint Lazarus' Day, a celebration of the passing winter and the renaissance of nature during the spring time.

This work is planned to be a mobile structure, which goes round and sways in its upper part.

The silhouette of the sculpture reminds me of a female figure, symbolizing the maternity and fertility of mother nature. The image of this wooden figure possesses some typical elements of the old Bulgarian architecture.

76

# ROBERT KOENIG

## Private Meeting
### 1981

My general plan was to find a site with fallen trees nearby. The sculpture was thus created and sited close to the original source of timber.

"Private Meeting" is a group of three standing figures carved in oak. This group helps to create a more complete environment on the theme of Ancestral Man, forest dweller - where the forest itself was a source for food gathering, tool and weapon making, shelter etc.

78

# SIMON LEE

### Solid Oak
#### 1991

"Solid Oak" juxtaposes two materials - the processed end product of the forest with the living trees. Part of Grizedale's beauty comes from it being a working forest, planted and harvested by man. It is a beauty created by the tension of two circumstances, the complex rythmn of the forest, and our equally complex manipulation of them.

I returned the chairs to the forest because they are a mirror and a support to the human form and can be seen as caricatures of it. The trees are young and will continue growing, shedding their leaves and branches over the years. The chairs will also fall piece by piece to the ground, changing the patterns imposed upon them, and becoming once again a part of the undergrowth that regenerates the forest.

80

# PATRICIA LEIGHTON

### Silurian Cant
### 1986

I have explored a continued interest in neolithic ceremonial sites, intrigued by the potent atmosphere they exude.

I intended with "Silurian Cant" to make a work which felt as if it purposefully belonged to its placing in the landscape, emitting a sense of timelessness. I chose an open site in a deciduous area of the forest which has two approaches on the Silurian Trail. It was important to retain the intimate qualities of Scale Green, and the oak, rowan and larch trees, without disrupting their natural balance. There is a quiet presence in this area, suggesting a meeting place of old, a place to spend time.

The works are situated in a ritualistic sequence while relating to the distant hills, Long Crag. I worked carefully with the scale of the four works in relation to their siting.

Above: Woven sculpture (1986)

# KARL LEWIS

**Standing Stone**
1991

"Standing Stone". A contemporary monument which reflects the region as it is and refers to its ancient/celtic past, to henges, stones circles, burial, the passing of time and it's effects. It is made from materials found in the forest and surrounding areas. Materials that have been through production processes, to become tools of work or shelter from the elements, and are now discarded.

84

# ZOE DE L'ISLE WHITTIER

### Meridian Owl
### 1993

As we move through the woods, unseen birds and animals watch us.

Early one morning, the ground covered in frost, Ash leaves fell all around me as I carved my stone. I picked one up and drew it on the stone's side.

This sculpture beckons one silently to the place where I feel a sense of calm.

86

# SALLY MATTHEWS

### Wolves
#### 1993

In 1993 I was able to make "Wolves". There was a site at Grizedale, a large sloping outcrop of slate with views over the valley. It's a wonderful site especially when the mist is down, or when the rocks steam in the sun. The perfect place for wolves to gather before a hunt.

# EMMA POSEY

## Omphalus
### 1993

Walking through the forest I was attracted to the areas of coniferous trees, their tall vertical trunks and their mottled light streaking through the branches - the warm colour of the needles carpeting the ground. The atmosphere created had a strong presence.

I wanted to build a rounded, smooth structure in contrast to the vertical trunks and imagined the beginnings of the trees as nuts and cones with their curves and folds.

I found myself echoing the hills and valleys. The terrain is a container for the lakes, like a boat is also a vessel.

I hope people explore the structure and use it as a base to observe the space around. I want the shapes to complement the forest, to sit quietly amongst the trees.

# ALANNAH ROBINS

### Ban an t - ishka
*Woman of the Water*
1995

During my time in Grizedale, one of the two women I was carving became a man. This was part of an important work process that allows the work to evolve in the making, involving an interaction of sculptor, site and materials.

Whilst the woman here is more actively giving, this is no battle of strengths. Both stand in the water, one baptizing, and the other being baptized.

Above: "Ban an T-ishka" *(detail)*

92

# BELLE SHAFIR

### The Seers' Well
#### 1994

Wouldn't we all like to know our future? I know I would.

The mysteries of the well, at the depths of which mysterious things take place, may hold an answer that might slowly float up to the surface towards me through the still water covered with moss.

The three figures represent me as Mother, Woman and Artist. They also might be the figures that will come to understand the meaning of the mysteries of the well, although I have not.

94

# KEIR SMITH

## Seven Stones Before the Old Man
### 1982

The sculpture overlooks the Grizedale valley. The highest local peak, the Old Man of Coniston, is seen in the distance. The work is in two parts, a pallisade of larch logs cut to the shape of the mountain, and in front of this, a row of seven "rocks" carved from wood. One rock, the largest, contains a deep reservoir filled with metal powder. This "Quarry stone" refers to the metal workings in Coppermines valley which leads to the summit of the Old Man. The remaining rocks have implement shapes cut into their top surfaces. On the right of the Quarry stone, axe, nail and sickle, on the left, spear, sword and arrow. These shapes are ghosts of potential within the metal ore. They were suggested by Bronze-Age flat moulds from the British Museum.

# SHIGEO TOYA

## God of Thunder - 4
### 1995

Pain accompanies anger. The Thunder-god in pain makes a wry face. Pain is transmitted to a tree in a fusion with the Thunder-god. The allegorical tree is full of death and yet beautiful. The tree that is handed down in stories. A signpost that leads to the other end of the door.

98

# KIMIO TSUCHIYA

## Stone Forest
### 1991

The stone forms the ground.

The ground supports the tree.

The tree create fresh water.

The water gives life.

The man becomes one and coexists with the continuity and the balance of nature. The nature become the spring of man. The sculpture stands motionless, reflects the time and the silent voice.

# ROSALIND WATES

### Grizedale Mosaic
### 1992

In the landscape, of the landscape, about the landscape. This is the theme of the Grizedale Mosaic, which lies part way up the east side of the Grizedale valley. The slowly evolving art of mosaic stretches back thousands of years.

The Grizedale Mosaic is an attempt at further exploration of the medium. My past mosaics have been constructed from man-made vitreous and ceramic pieces, but the Grizedale Society which commissioned this work gave me the opportunity to investigate the use of natural, local materials.

The mosaic has an unashamedly environmental theme. Five indigenous mammals frozen mid-movement and turned to stone follow each other around the central sun. Balancing this fiery heart is another element essential to life: a river motif, which forms a border to the mosaic.

Many of the sculptures at Grizedale reflect the passing of time, the transience of the seasons. Made from organic materials, they exist for a while, then decay naturally back into the ground; a planned mortality which is an essential part of their concept. The Grizedale Mosaic is different.  As the Romans left their mark, so have I left mine: a message to future generations saying that we didn't just care about wealth, power, and the materialistic things of life; beyond all that, there's a part of us that is still claimed by the wilderness.

# FORESTRY AND ART

## BRIAN MAHONY

Grizedale is a unique forest. Its long history of management dates back to the time when, after the Norman Conquest, the woodlands were granted to the monks of Furness Abbey who valued them for many purposes : for hunting; as provider of fodder for pigs and other livestock; as a source of timber for building; and for coppice wood to provide charcoal for iron smelting and a myriad of other items as diverse as barrels and baskets. The woodlands were seen to have a value. They provided for the needs of the local economy and were a place of employment for people.

Although changing over time, the uses of the forest have sustained it through to the present. Careful nurture and management by generations of foresters have ensured that in the late twentieth Century, we still have a thriving and vibrant forest at Grizedale which, in the same way as the forest of the Middle Ages met the needs of the monastic community, can provide for the expectations and needs of people today.

The forest is dynamic and it is much more than simply trees, although these are present in great number and variety through the ancient oakwoods, the ornamental mixed woodlands planted by the Victorians, to the more recently established spruce, larch and fir. The other key elements of the forest resource which help to make up its interest and complexity include plantlife, animals and insects; physical features such as rock, soil and water; access routes; open space, including the agricultural land; buildings; historical features; and, very importantly, people - either residents, workers or visitors. Begin to add all of these features together and one quickly recognises the immense potential which the forest holds. Add to them, the more abstract qualities of solitude; remoteness, closeness to nature; legend and mystery, and all manner of possibilities open up.

As managers of the forest, we need to work creatively with all of its attributes and to carefully balance them so that the forest can meet today's needs, but at the same time be sustained for the benefit of future generations. Grizedale is in public ownership. It is managed on behalf of the public by Forest Enterprise to provide timber for our daily needs; to provide opportunities for quiet recreation; to conserve wild life and historic features; and to do all of this in a way which is sensitive to its place in the landscape of the Lake District National Park.

There is also the added magical ingredient of the arts in a magnificent forest setting. Sculpture, painting, performance and crafts all find a home at Grizedale through the unique partnership with the Grizedale Society. Through its close relationship with Forest Enterprise, the Society has been able to unlock the potential of the forest to provide inspiration to artists and to make art accessible for the visitor in a way which enhances their experience and enjoyment of the forest. Whilst foresters manage the woodlands and their wildlife, and build and waymark access routes for walkers and cyclists, the Grizedale Society is able to encourage artists to make use of the resource to create sculpture which interprets and enhances the forest for the benefit of all, perhaps in the process reinvoking some of the mystery and drama that has inevitably ebbed away over time with the loss of the wildwood.

The close relationship between the Grizedale Society and Forest Enterprise means that Forest Craftsmen might find themselves using their skills in helping to transport and erect an intricately carved tree trunk, working with a Japanese sculptor who has no English, whilst planning of harvesting or felling operations will often involve detailed measures to protect or accommodate a woodland sculpture.

Management must approach the forest in an holistic way which does not allow one aspect to dominate. Each aspect adds its contribution to the total of products, values and experiences which the forest provides, in a way which is not discordant, and which ensures that the integrity and value of the forest is always sustained for the future.

Grizedale is not simply a timber factory; or a sculpture park; or a wildlife reserve; or a public playground. Through the efforts of foresters and artists working closely together, it is in part all of these.